For my own talented builders of traps –
Wil, Leanna and Ben

Leanna
and the
Genie Trap

Story Hazel Hutchins
Pictures Catharine O'Neill

Oxford University Press

The day Leanna lost the most important piece in her entire building block set her mother said, 'If you had put everything away safe and sound in the box it wouldn't be lost.'

But Leanna knew that wasn't why the part was missing at all.

It was missing because of the genie.

The genie looked like Leanna's Uncle Lawrence, except the genie had a long, black liquorice-whip moustache. His picture was painted on the blue tin box that Leanna and her mother had bought at a garage sale. They had also bought a used sofa and an old chest of drawers.

Since the day the blue box had come home with them, Leanna's mother had lost her wrist watch and her favourite pen. Aunt Laurel had lost her red crochet hook. Leanna's dad had lost a pair of pliers. The baby had lost two dummies, and Leanna had lost her best hair-slides, her favourite rock, and the single most important piece in her entire building block set.

Leanna decided there was only one thing to do.

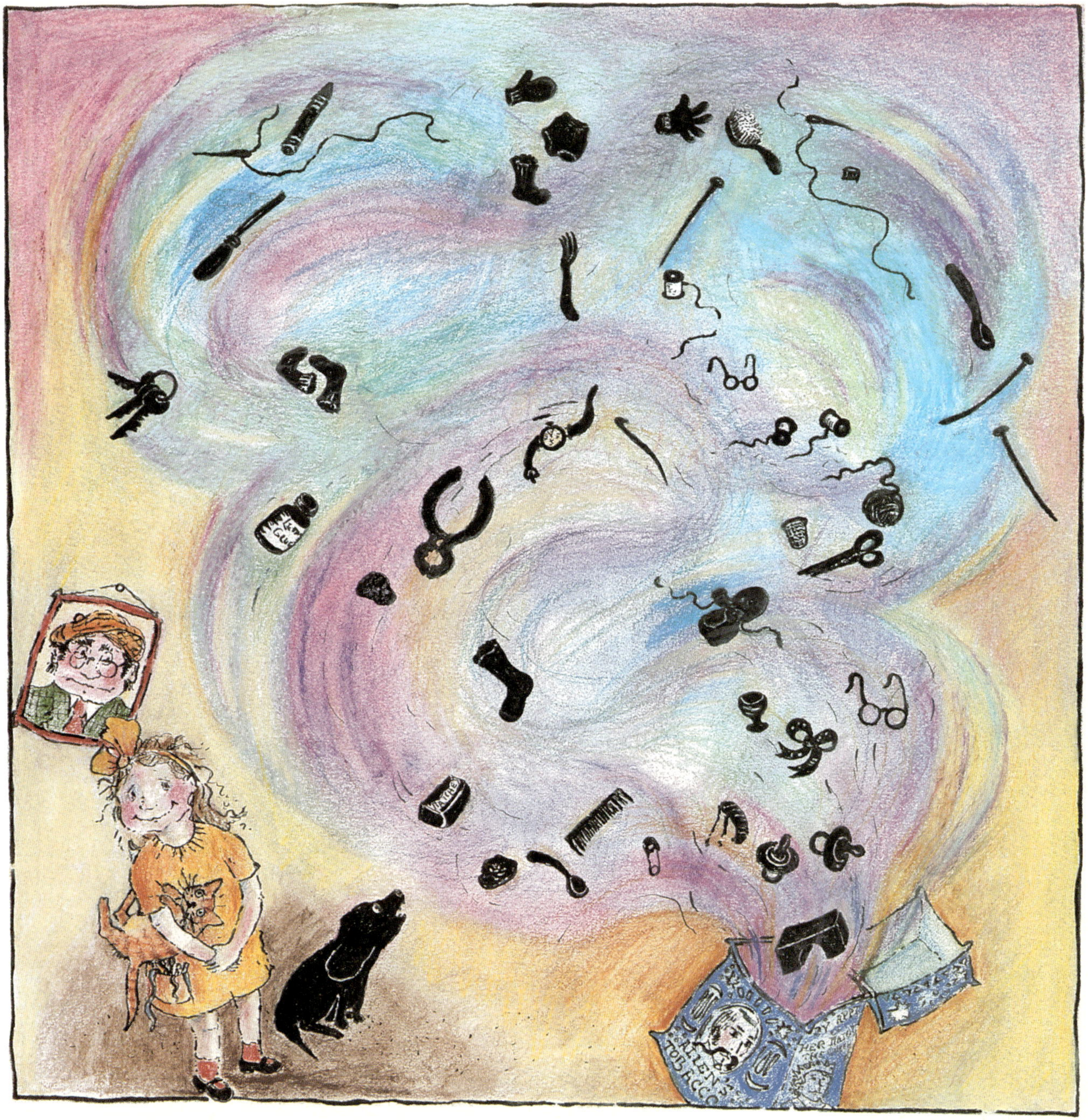
ALLEN'S

She made the trap out of two blankets, one box, the tie from an old dressing gown, a long ruler, two pairs of shoe laces and a lump of playdough. For bait she used her favourite ring. She waited in her room for three hours and when she was about to give up she caught the genie.

It was shorter than she had expected and made very odd noises and it turned out to be her baby brother, Norman. She knew he wasn't the genie. Norman only stole things he could eat.

Leanna learned from her mistake. She realised she couldn't build a proper blanket trap because she didn't know exactly what size the genie was. She borrowed the old camera with the big flash and used three pairs of shoe laces and a bit of string to trip the trigger. She left it all set up when she went to bed that night.

Except that didn't work either.

This only made Leanna more determined. She went downstairs and looked at her father's tools for a long time. Then she went to talk to her mother.

'Please may I saw a hole in the floor to make a trap-door to catch the genie?' asked Leanna.

Leanna's mother was kind, intelligent, and multi-talented but she was sometimes not as imaginative as Leanna would have liked her to be.

'No,' said Leanna's mother.

Leanna went into the living room to sulk. She was not very good at sulking – it was too boring. She wasn't very good at sitting either. She made her skipping rope into a large snare loop. She spread it out in the middle of the living room floor. She disguised it well. She hid herself beneath the cushions on the next-to-new sofa. And while she was waiting there to catch the genie . . .

. . . the sofa grabbed her by the foot!

'Let go,' said Leanna and pulled.

'Let go,' said Leanna and pushed.

'Let go,' said Leanna and twisted around until she was upside down and backwards.

'No,' said the sofa.

'Sofas can't talk,' said Leanna.

The sofa said nothing, but it didn't let go either. Leanna stopped pulling. She decided to think things out. Very carefully she wiggled her toes. Her foot was caught in a little pocket that ran along the back of the sofa beneath the cushions. And it was not alone in there. There were other things too – hard metallic things, pointy plastic things, smooth rubbery ones.

'Are you collecting things in there?' asked Leanna suspiciously.

'What if I am?' said the sofa.

'Look,' said Leanna, who knew all about collecting things. 'Feet are not good for collecting. They're too big and sometimes smelly and they're attached to bodies that need to run around.'

'I'm listening,' said the sofa.

Leanna felt in her pockets. As usual, she had quite a collection on hand herself.

'Maybe we can work something out,' said Leanna.

Leanna traded a ladybird fridge magnet for the release of her left foot. She traded half a stick of chewing gum for her mother's watch and then she traded the world's smallest yo-yo (which didn't actually work but had a very nice feel to it), for the single most important piece in her entire building block set.

'Friends?' asked Leanna as she slipped the yo-yo into the pocket at the back of the sofa.

'Friends,' agreed the sofa as it spit up her building block.

There is no genie living in Leanna's house, but their sofa still steals things. Whenever it takes something that someone really likes or really needs, Leanna goes and quietly trades to get it back. She lets the sofa keep the other treasures. It is a very trustworthy sofa and things are as safe with it as anywhere.

And sometimes, when she is buried deep in one of her caves beneath the sofa cushions, Leanna will hear a low rumbly-clinky-shuffly noise. It is the sound of the sofa sorting through its collection and humming in a most contented manner.

Oxford University Press, Walton Street, Oxford OX2 6DP
Oxford New York Toronto
Delhi Bombay Calcutta Madras Karachi
Petaling Jaya Singapore Hong Kong Tokyo
Nairobi Dar es Salaam Cape Town
Melbourne Auckland

and associated companies in
Beirut Berlin Ibadan Nicosia

Oxford is a trade mark of Oxford University Press

Text © 1986 H.J. Hutchins
Illustration © 1986 Catharine O'Neill
First published in Canada by Annick Press Ltd., Toronto
First published in the U.K. by Oxford University Press 1987

British Library Cataloguing in Publication Data
Hutchins, Hazel J.
   Leanna and the genie trap.
   I. Title II. O'Neill, Catharine
   813' .54 [J]   PZ7
   ISBN 0 19 279859 6

Typeset by PGT Graphic Design, Oxford
Printed in Canada